C000157343

All Woman
volume one

Compiled by Mark Mumford and Carole Staff
Published 1994

© International Music Publications Limited
Southend Road, Woodford Green, Essex IG8 8HN, England
Reproducing this music in any form is illegal and forbidden by the Copyright, Designs and Patents Act 1988
215-2-1098

ALL WOMAN

Words and Music by
STANSFIELD, DEVANEY and MORRIS

© 1991 Big Life Music Ltd., London W1N 5DE

4

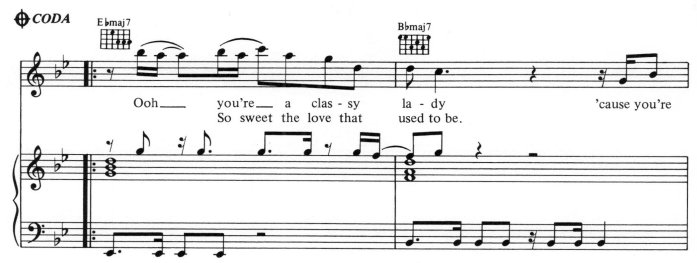

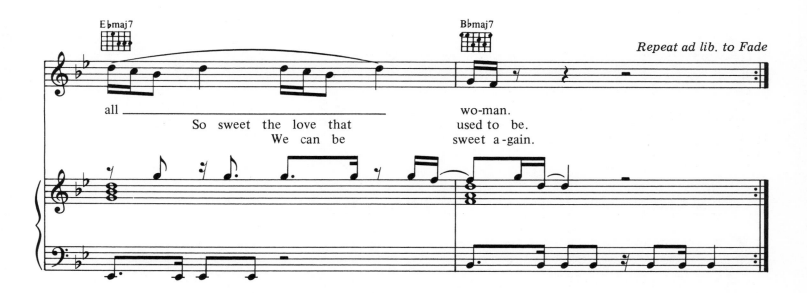

VERSE 2:
She stands there and lets the tears flow
Tears that she's been holding back so long
She wonders where did all the loving go
The love they used to share when they were strong.

She says yes, I look a mess
But I don't love you any less
I thought you always thought enough of me
To always be impressed.

CHORUS 2:
I may not be a lady
But I'm all woman
From Monday to Sunday I work my fingers to the bone
I'm no classy lady
But I'm all woman
This woman needs a little love to make her strong
You're not the only one.

VERSE 3:
He holds her and hangs his head in shame
He doesn't see her like he used to do
He's too wrapped up in working for his pay
He hasn't seen the pain he's put her through.

Attention that he paid
Just vanished in the haze
He remembers how it used to be
When he used to say.

CHORUS 3:
You'll always be a lady
'Cause you're all woman
From Monday to Sunday I love you much more than you know
You're a classy lady
'Cause you're all woman
This woman needs a loving man to keep her warm.

CABARET

Words by FRED EBB
Music by JOHN KANDER

© 1966 Alley Music Corp./Trio Music Co. Inc., U.S.A.
Carlin Music Corp., London NW1 8BD

8

GET HERE

Words and Music by
BRENDA RUSSELL

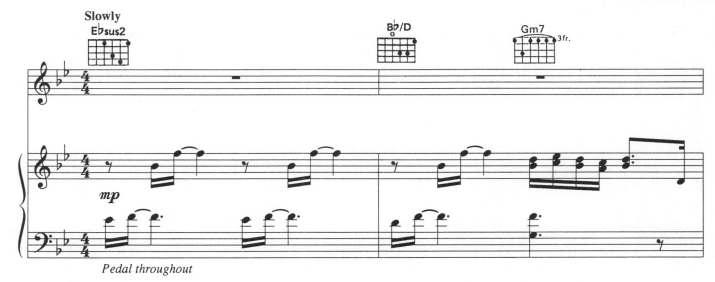

Pedal throughout

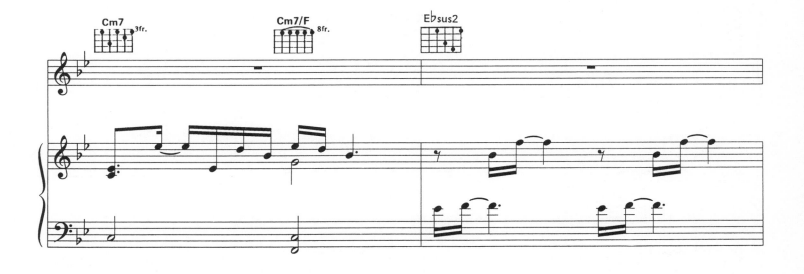

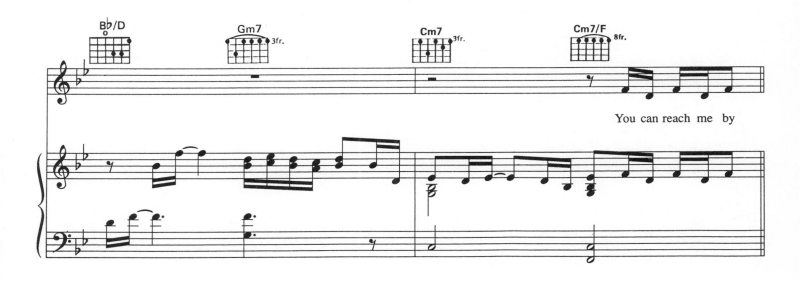

You can reach me by

© 1988 Rutland Road Music
Warner Chappell Music Ltd., London W1Y 3FA

I don't care

how you get here, just get here if you can.

CAN'T STAY AWAY FROM YOU

Words and Music by
GLORIA ESTEFAN

© 1987 Foreign Imported Productions & Publishing, Inc., USA
EMI Songs Ltd., London WC2H 0EA

Don't wan-na be in your way,_____
how much you need me too,_____

and I don't wan-na be your_____ sec-ond choice;
though you're leav-ing me no_____ oth-er choice

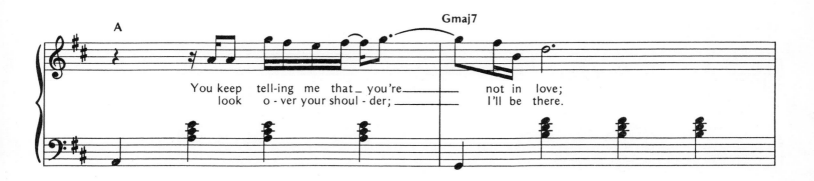

don't wan-na be just your friend._____
than to turn and walk a - way,_____

You keep tell-ing me that you're_____ not in love;
look o - ver your shoul-der;_____ I'll be there.

you wan-na throw it all a - way._____
You can count on me to stay._____

DO YOU KNOW WHERE YOU'RE GOING TO?

Words by GERRY GOFFIN
Music by MIKE MASSER

© 1973 Screen Gems-EMI Music Inc. and Jobete Music Co. Inc., U.S.A.
Screen Gems-EMI Music Ltd., London WC2H 0EA

Why must—we wait so long — be - fore we see

how sad the ans - wers to those ques - tions can be?—

know?

Coda

23

ETERNAL FLAME

Words and Music by
BILLY STEINBERG, TOM KELLY
and SUSANNA HOFFS

© 1988, 1989 Billy Steinberg Music, Denise Barry Music,
EMI Blackwood Music Inc., & Bangophile Music, USA
Warner Chappell Music Ltd., London W1Y 3FA/EMI Songs Ltd., London WC2H 0EA

EV'RY TIME WE SAY GOODBYE

Words and Music
by COLE PORTER

© 1944 Chappell & Co. Inc. U.S.A.
Warner Chappell Music Ltd., London W1Y 3FA

FEVER

Words and Music by
JOHN DAVENPORT
and EDDIE COOLEY

© 1956 Jay and Cee Music Corp., assigned to Fort Knox Music Co., U.S.A.
Lark Music Ltd., London NW1 8BD

Additional Verses

Verse 3: Romeo loved Juliet,
Juliet she felt the same.
When he put his arms around her, he said,
"Julie, baby you're my flame."

Chorus: Thou givest fever, when we kisseth
FEVER with thy flaming youth.
FEVER – I'm afire
FEVER, yea I burn forsooth.

Verse 4: Captain Smith and Pocahantas
Had a very mad affair
When her Daddy tried to kill him, she said,
"Daddy-o don't you dare."

Chorus: Give me fever, with his kisses,
FEVER when he holds me tight.
FEVER – I'm his Missus
Oh Daddy won't you treat him right.

Verse 5: Now you've listened to my story
Here's the point that I have made.
Chicks were born to give you FEVER
Be it fahreheit or centigrade.

Chorus: They give you FEVER, when you kiss them
FEVER if you live and learn.
FEVER – till you sizzle
What a lovely way to burn.

THE GREATEST LOVE OF ALL

Words by LINDA CREED
Music by MICHAEL MASSER

© 1977 Gold Horizon Music Corp. and Golden Torch Music Corp., USA
EMI Music Publishing Ltd., London WC2H 0EA

I AM WHAT I AM

Words and Music by
JERRY HERMAN

© 1983 Jerry Herman, Jerryco Music Co. and Edwin H. Morris & Co. Inc., USA
Chappell Morris Ltd., LondonW1Y 3FA

I ONLY WANT TO BE WITH YOU

Words and Music by
MIKE HAWKER
and IVOR RAYMONDE

© 1963 Chappell Music Ltd., London W1Y 3FA

LIKE A PRAYER

Words and Music by
MADONNA CICCONE
and PAT LEONARD

© 1989 WB Music Corp., Bleu Disque Music Co. Inc., Webo Girl Publishing, Inc. & Johnny Yuma Music, USA
Warner Chappell Music Ltd., London W1Y 3FA

MISS YOU LIKE CRAZY

Words and Music by
PRESTON GLASS, MICHAEL MASSER
and GERRY GOFFIN

© 1989 Irving Music Inc., Gemid Music, Screen Gems-EMI Music Inc. and Prince Street Music, USA
Rondor Music (London) Ltd., London SW6 4TW, Screen Gems-EMI Music Ltd. London WC2H 0EA and
Chelsea Music Publishing Co. Ltd., London W1H 4AJ

Chorus:

I miss you like— cra - zy,— I miss you like— cra - zy,

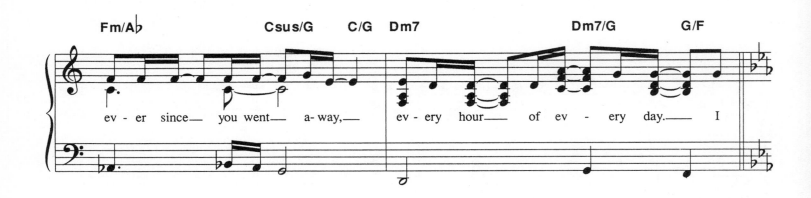

ev - er since— you went— a - way,— ev - ery hour— of ev - ery day.— I

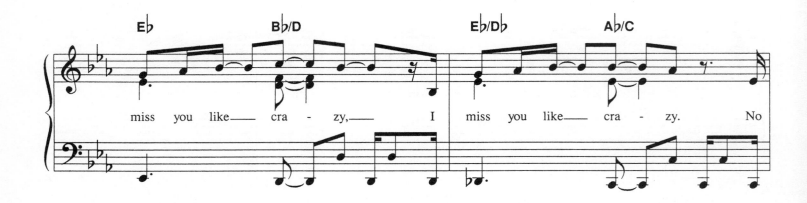

miss you like— cra - zy,— I miss you like— cra - zy. No

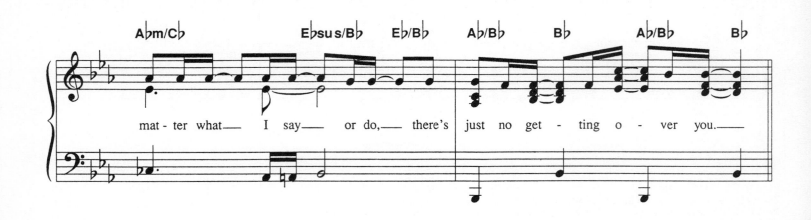

mat - ter what— I say— or do,— there's just no get - ting o - ver you.—

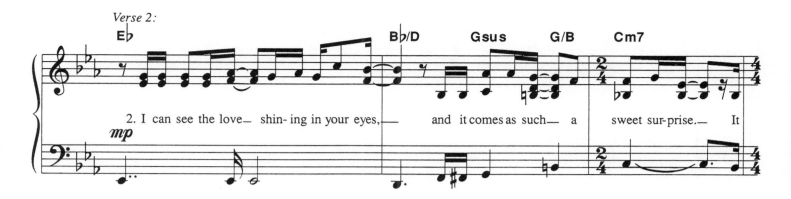

Verse 2:

2. I can see the love— shin-ing in your eyes,— and it comes as such— a sweet sur-prise.— It

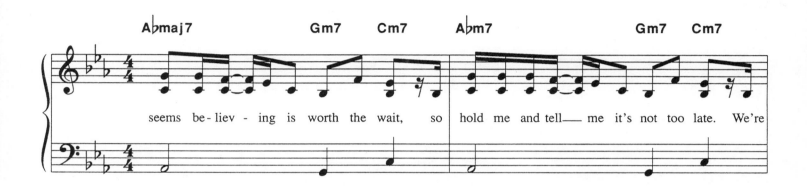

seems be - liev - ing is worth the wait, so hold me and tell— me it's not too late. We're

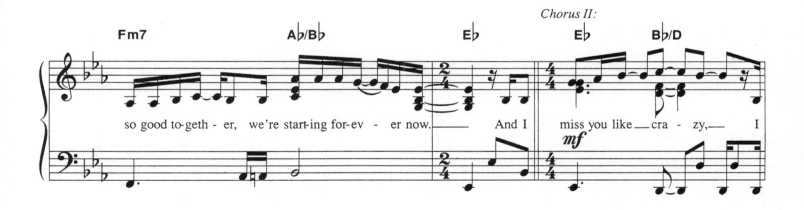

so good to-geth - er, we're start-ing for-ev - er now.— And I miss you like— cra - zy,— I

Chorus II:

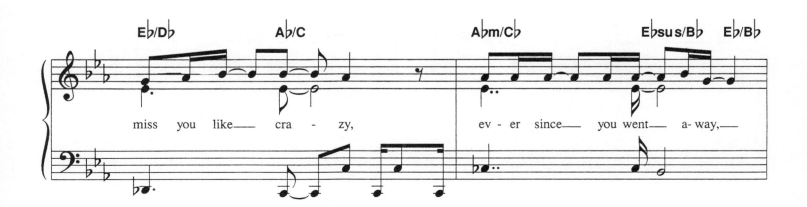

miss you like— cra - zy, ev - er since— you went— a-way,—

I WILL ALWAYS LOVE YOU

Words and Music by
DOLLY PARTON

© 1973 Velvet Apple Music, USA
Carlin Music Corp., London NW1 8BD

Verse 3: Instrumental solo

Verse 4:
I hope life treats you kind
And I hope you have all you've dreamed of.
And I wish to you, joy and happiness.
But above all this, I wish you love.
(To Chorus:)

NOBODY DOES IT BETTER

Words by CAROLE BAYER SAGER
Music by MARVIN HAMLISCH

© 1977 United Artists Music Co. Inc.,USA
EMI United Partnership Ltd., London WC2H 0EA

OVER THE RAINBOW

Words by E.Y. HARBURG
Music by HAROLD ARLEN

*Dorothy - Judy Garland

© 1938 EMI Feist Catalog, Inc./EMI Catalogue Partnership, USA
EMI United Partnership Ltd., London WC2H 0EA

THE ROSE

Words and Music by
AMANDA McBROOM

© 1977 Fox Fanfare Music Inc.
Warner Chappell Music Ltd., London W1Y 3FA

SAVE THE BEST FOR LAST

Words and Music by
PHIL GALDSTON, JON LIND
and WENDY WALDMAN

© 1989 Moon and Stars Music, Longitude Music, Windswept Pacific, Big Mystique Music,
Kazzoom Music Inc. and Virgin Songs., USA
EMI Virgin Music Ltd., London WC2H 0EA, Windswept Pacific Music, London W11 3EP and
Warner Chappell Music Ltd., London W1Y 3FA

It's not the way ___ I hoped ___ or ___ how ___
Some - times the ver - y thing ___ you're ___ look

___ I planned, ___ but some - how it's e - nough. ___
- ing for ___ is the one thing you can't see. ___

And now we're stand - ing face ___ to face. ___
But now we're stand - ing face ___ to face. ___

Is - n't this world ___ a cra - zy place? ___

Just when I thought _____ our chance_ had passed,_

_ you go and save ____ the best ___ for last. _

All of the nights _____

SUMMERTIME

Words by DU BOSE HEYWARD
Music by GEORGE GERSHWIN

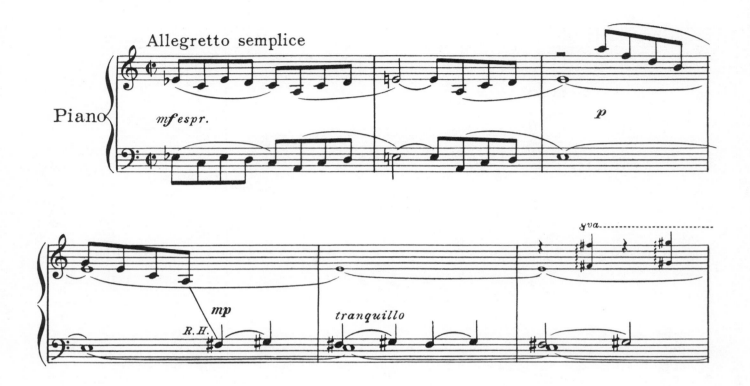

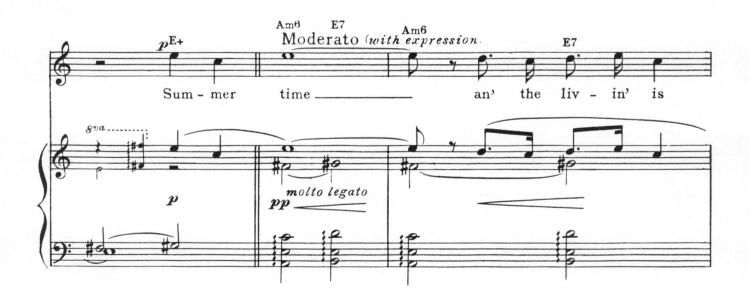

© 1935 Gershwin Publishing Corp./Chappell & Co. Inc., U.S.A.
Warner Chappell Music Ltd., London W1Y 3FA

SUPERWOMAN

Words and Music by
BABY FACE, L.A. REID
and D. SIMMONS

© 1982 Kear Music, Green Skirt Music and Epic Solar Songs Inc., USA
Warner Chappell Music Ltd., London W1Y 3FA

kind of girl, that can treat you so sweet, but you've got to re - a-lise that you've got to be sweet-er to me.

I need

love, I need just __ your __ love. _____ I'm not your

D.S. Chorus to Fade

SHOUT

Words and Music by
O'KELLY ISLEY, RONALD ISLEY
and RUDOLPH ISLEY

© 1959, 1962 Big Seven Music Corp. and Wemar Music Corp., U.S.A.
George Wiener Music Ltd., London NW4 2EF

WHY DO FOOLS FALL IN LOVE

Words and Music by
FRANK LYMON and GEORGE GOLDNER

© 1956 Patricia Music Publishing Corp. USA
Warner Chappell Music Ltd., London W1Y 3FA

WHAT'S LOVE GOT TO DO WITH IT

Words and Music by
GRAHAM LYLE and TERRY BRITTEN

© 1984 Myaxe Music Ltd., WB Music Corp and Good Single Ltd., USA
Warner Chappell Music Ltd., London W1Y 3FA and Rondor Music (London) Ltd., London SW6 4TW

THE WAY WE WERE

Words by ALAN BERGMAN
and MARILYN BERGMAN
Music by MARVIN HAMLISCH

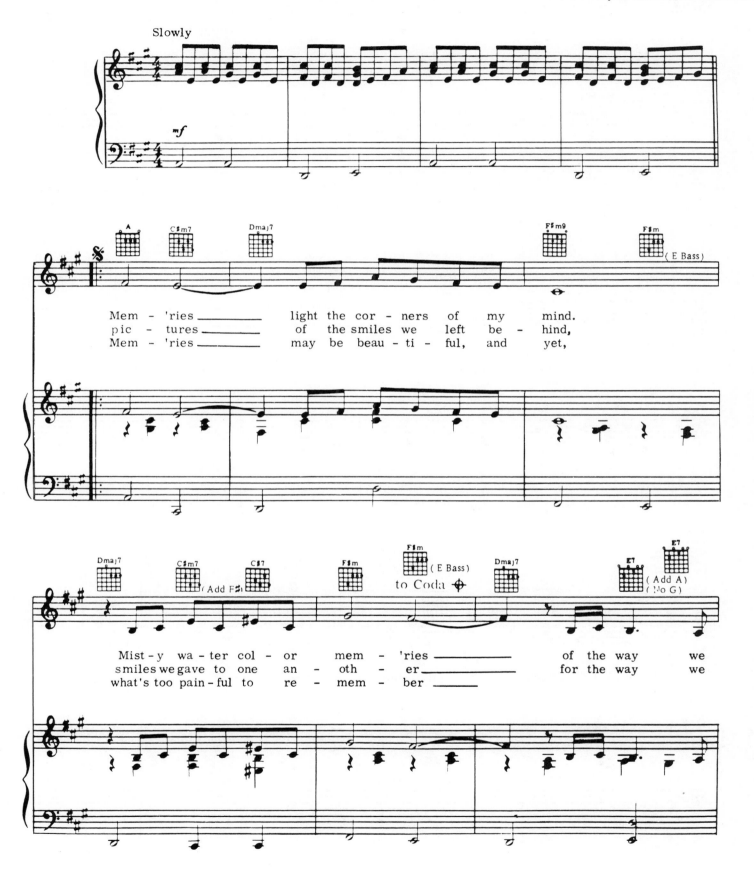

© 1973 Screen Gems-EMI Music, London WC2H 0EA

Coda

we sim-ply choose to for - get.   So it's the

laugh - ter   we will re - mem - ber, _____ _____ when-ev - er we re - mem - ber _____ the way we

were;   The way we were. _____

Reproduced and printed by
Halstan & Co. Ltd., Amersham, Bucks., England